The Undertow

The Undertow

Emily Bilman

Copyright © 2023 Emily Bilman

The moral right of the author has been asserted.

Apart from any fair dealing for the purposes of research or private study, or criticism or review, as permitted under the Copyright, Designs and Patents Act 1988, this publication may only be reproduced, stored or transmitted, in any form or by any means, with the prior permission in writing of the publishers and the author, or in the case of reprographic reproduction in accordance with the terms of licences issued by the Copyright Licensing Agency. Enquiries concerning reproduction outside those terms should be sent to the publishers and the author. All other inquiries should be sent to the author.

Matador
Unit E2 Airfield Business Park,
Harrison Road, Market Harborough,
Leicestershire. LE16 7UL
Tel: 0116 2792299
Email: books@troubador.co.uk
Web: www.troubador.co.uk/matador
Twitter: @matadorbooks

ISBN 978 1805140 153

British Library Cataloguing in Publication Data.
A catalogue record for this book is available from the British Library.

Printed in the UK by TJ Books, Padstow, Cornwall
Typeset in 13pt Aldine401 BT by Troubador Publishing Ltd, Leicester, UK

Matador is an imprint of Troubador Publishing Ltd

Table of Contents

THE UNDERTOW	1
Hubris	3
The Causeway	4
The Undertow	5
Despondency	6
On the Isthmus	7
The Sea-League	8
Dispossession	9
Challenger	10
Revoked	11
Immunity	12
Fragments	13
Time	14
The Camera	16
Chalk-Hills	17
Sunbathers	18
Summer	19
The Sea-Sigh	20
A Marine Heart	21
Pathfinder	22
Barrier-Skin	23
The Warrants	24
THE SCAVENGER-MOON	25
The Scavenger-Moon	27
Scavenger-Lover	28
Horizon	29
The Convict	30
Tsunami	31
Actors and Alibis	32
Disjuncture	33
Guilt	34
Disbelief	35
Life-Force	37

The Landmark	38
Balsam	39
Love's Ally	40
Metamorphosis	41
Dispossession	42
The Body-Dam	43
THE RAFT	45
The Raft	47
The Mask in Sutton Hoo	48
The Albatross	49
Cod-Roe	50
The Life-Tree	51
The Dunes	52
A Maritime Battle	53
Synchronicity	54
Ambidextrous	55
The Whale's Cradle	56
The Whale-Way	57
Blind Spots	58
The Abalone Hunt	59
Glimpses of Light	60
Chiaroscuro	61
The Lightkeeper	62
Acknowledgements	63
Author's Biography	65

The Undertow

Hubris

Like a sea-sentinel, she refused
to abandon her self-assigned field.
From their dinghy they dumped
their pride and all its deceitful tributaries

to the Aegean. Standing on the receding gate
he said pride was all they possessed.
Confined and distanced from her loved ones
she remained attached to him.

They travelled through undertows
through highways lit at dawn
moved countries and were bound

to be severed through water, land,
and vennel enigmas, through that cryptic
entanglement of river-rhizomes.

The Causeway

I walked along a concrete causeway
and imagined the river's umber alluvium
oozing into the sea languidly while
the mineral-sea fermented the waters
like yeast in bread-dough rising.

The wind-swept shifting sands moved
among the sepia dunes. The day's drought
and the wind scorched my transpired skin.

Across the dunes, the delta-fields spurted
into the glochids of the golden echinocactus
seeded in symmetrical twin-rows.

Above me flew a golden flock of orioles
migrating towards the southern desert
abundant in scorpions, beetles, and bats.

I saw those fledgling flights in rhythms
of evolving patterns to stave off predators.
Like the shaping spirit brooding on the causeway
the golden swarms in flight carried
subdued sequels of ancestral wisdom.

The Undertow

In halcyon days when oak leaves whisper
to the breeze, breathing is serene,
contrary to stress-filled days when the breath
gets constrained on the throat-tunnel
like a large dam safeguarding indolent
waters. Like the river's kelp-swung undertow
on calm days, the breath leaves the lungs
settling down to its own unconscious rhythm.

Like a tributary flowing into the river
intuition opens the breath cavity leading
to a well-spring of meaning. Like scribes
bent upon papyrus we read and re-read
the words written with a sombre calligraphy
until poems are welded like argosies.

Despondency

The sun-disk, illuminating the beryl-beach,
an illusion, perhaps, broken by a crystal tide,
spurred me towards sunlight. The transformative
quest of my childhood regenerated my dreams.

In irony, the troubled gaze of your melancholy
announced the sudden loss of your leather diary.
In the high tide of our encounter, I read
The Prelude fluently yet, with the dusk,

the verses waned into the dim shadows
of your despondency. I cried and cried out
my eyes' moons each time you departed.

When the new moon turned into a silver crescent
despite the switched lights, we both felt dejected.

On the Isthmus

So, Odysseus stepped onto his ship
And entered Oceanus, the land's mythic
Fluvial girdle. As he crossed their seas
He warred against the giant Cyclops,
Daring to traverse their danger-routes.

Surreptitiously, the sirens threw
Boulders towards him, blocking
The straits. Odysseus thwarted
The spectre-sirens who destroyed
The sailors' desire for women
Deceiving them with their dithyrambs.

Fiery Charybdis schemed, spewed
Ogre-swathes of water and swallowed
The stranded ship. Nude, he hung onto a branch.
Six sailors were ceded to Scylla
Who immediately consumed them all.
So, Odysseus saved his sea-faring ship.

The Sea-League

Pilgrims tread softly on sleek
pine-needles until the brick house,
anointed with frankincense,
suspires with candle-wax.

The diva, in the hearth-shaped
amphitheatre under the crescent moon,
with the perfect pitch for expensive
ballads, sang about her prime *provocateur.*

The chorus on stage sang their lunar
journey of loess, rust, and brine.

The commercial nexus, founded
by a sacrificial Amazon had
moved west with the silted river.

Austere, the pines, scenting resin-balm
celebrated the fledgling sea-league.

Coins were carved on electrum
to revere the effigy of the deity,
her marble breast-emblems,
warrants of the city's perennity.

Shore to shore, nobles, and traders
chanted an Aegean eulogy.

Dispossession

Like Orpheus, Lot's anonymous
wife refuses divine advice, looks
back and sees the city of sin
perhaps seeking her kith and kin.

At the exit, she becomes a salt-statue
a rock eroded by wind and brine.

>An elder prophet pleading to God
>with *chutzpah* and humility
>negotiating   on account
>of the very innocent few
>fails to save   the uncouth city.

Lot's unnamed wife loses
her daft daughters to incest
to multiply her husband's seeds.

The elder prophet leaves the land.

Dispossessed are we of our past initiations.

In the immensity of the void, angels
protect us and beckon us to progress.

Challenger

The engine dives yet deeper
Into Orpheus' dark subterranean
Trenches along volcanic vents
That spurt out obsidian gas-fumes
Where bacteria swarms thrive
Like bee-colonies in a wild prairie.

In these ice-waters, all sea-creatures
Are liquified but, on a layer above,
Lantern-fish gleam to prey, mate,
And maintain the primaeval breath
Of silence. Buried in tenebrous
Shadows matter aggregated
And darkness was abraded by light.

Revoked

Like sound-waves lapping upon halcyon
Sands, my mother-of-pearl necklace

handled as an heirloom, softly touches my skin.
My body becomes my ancestor's bitter host

a virtual shield that drives and defends me.
My skin endures fraud, lies, and ploys.

Despair is revoked.

Like light sifting through the dusk-clouds
like salt-water oozing through the sands

the ethereal ghost revives my intuition
borne through skin-to-skin intimacy.

Immunity

When I swim in the seas of my childhood
I feel my protective shadow as a shielding mask.

When I swim farther in the plankton-sea
I suddenly grow fearsome of my own shadow
that once struggled to drive away the swarms
and sly multitudes that tried to steal the serenity
of my childhood. As I dive to plankton-rich

depths the swarms disappear. Submarine sands
shiver with rainbow-wrasse. The iodine-waters
wadded with minerals swallow my anxiety.
When I swim towards the shore as a weightless
figure, juvenile fish-swarms reconcile me

with those who assailed my childhood cocoon
that kept my pupae-organs warm and immune.

Fragments

Within a few minutes the summer moon
hidden behind the clouds dissolves
my dream, the earth's twin-shadow.
The wind whispers my unconscious dream

to the child's shadow lost like a swan
on an alpine lake waiting for a sea-change.
Unkempt shadows linger across blurred frames
yet the sea unlocks my dream and swells

my imagination with ethereal patterns,
those broken thresholds. Well-framed, I draw
concentric circles on the tidal pools of mourning

reading, within a book, the life of a diplomat –
the candour of the enigmas, the internal fights –
those fragments of an unfinished memoir.

Time

A meditation

Would Time be an indivisible integral
dream made of inchoate fragments?
As the envelope of our life, Time
contains the fragments of our thoughts
that we remember and sometimes forget.

Like water-swathes, Time, I think,
contains the day's diverging hours.
When the halcyon breeze eases
my breath, Time, like marine iodine,
seems as organic as the sea.

The day becomes a *tabula rasa,*
the mind, a projective mirror, almost
an eye. After the day's contents, sleep
and dreams, rejuvenate the new day.

Dreams, like Time, the recollected
and the forgotten ones, clear the day's
remainders from their rubble.
Within the city's green apertures
our mind becomes a slate-shaft.

Like an egg holding its yolk, Time
remains integral in an ever-expanding
present, wide and tangible, a present
we do not wish to curtail nor stain
with the wrong ingredients.

Life's river begins to flow into transient currents.
The land yields fruit, barley, and corn.
The mind, awake in sustenance,
integrates dispersed dream-images.

Like the ocean's currents, the present
becomes the flow of self into self,
recognizing the other. The present
that contains us regenerates Time.

The Camera

I wondered by the river-bank as gulls shrieked
above me in the bright open sky while the heron
stood lonely upon the sand glimpsing at the fish
that jumped out of the water listlessly. The river

engorged with the melting snow continues
to flow towards the valley of vineyards
while I stand on the bridge, my mind a camera
that records the passage of the present

yet, remembers the still time of fluvial memories:
how we used to fish the silver-spotted trout
measure the length of its humid skin slipping
between our fingers, unhook its curved kype

then throw it back to the translucent waters
and rapidly swap our rain-soaked sweaters.

Chalk-Hills

The silk-chalk in the new-born bay feels
like soft talcum powder under our feet.

Like the wind-swirled primeval sands
under the mutinous seas, the grated chalk

powder in our hands is inodorous, yet
heals the open wounds in your hand. As we walk,

high waves gnaw the chalk-hills, shape
them into convex moons. Wind-gusts

sweep the seas as in creation day, sculpting
the limestone layers into sheer geometries

like the transient dust that shaped us
from minerals, iron, oxygen, and carbon.

Sunbathers

Sunbathers sprawled like sunflowers
on the beryl-beach. I swam away from
the shore with the song of the frozen fruit
vendors receding towards the sea.

What gait was mine in the open plasma-sea?

As my heft yielded to the teal water
I could feel my heartbeat as steady
as my breast strokes. Rejuvenated
by the swim my muscles tensed
as I climbed up the boat's sturdy stairs.

The ice-boxes would have been opened
on the maquis-sands – the water-melon,
coconuts and corn kept in dripping
thick ice, sold to the sunbathers.

Summer

The seas begin to swell
tides invade the porous rocks
crabs peep out of the gaps

A juvenile swan
draws concentric circles
on a tidal pool

Summer wind whispers
people run under canopies
rain opens the skies

Hidden behind clouds
the moon dissolves our shadows
dark drop by dark drop

The Sea-Sigh

The cerulean sea of the archipelago turned
lead-grey under the heft of the Leviathan trapped
in the lagoon. As daylight brightened the brick
towers and houses at dawn, I photographed

a thousand-ton cruise ship on the Adriatic.
Like pilgrims eager to absolve their reproaches
with music and masks, tourists rushed
to buy *papier mâché* masks. My bond

with the sea broken, I sighed with the bridges
linking the islands to the mainland. A resident said
ships will soon be mooring along the causeway
of the industrious city. In awe, I apprehended

the dissonance of the city's dependency
at odds with the residents' despondency.

A Marine Heart

The gilt-breams slide pass me
on the diaphanous waters, their lithe
dorsal fins bent down like folded sails
while I dive head-down into the salt-
water, blessing each liquid mineral ion
oozing into my skin, carrying me deep
into the depths, rendering me weightless.

As I swim back towards the shore, the gilt-
breams slither across the soft breaths
of the sea-sands, their silver-lamella
blending into their own transparencies –

their crimson phosphorescent gills
pumping the sea's liquid oxygen
like a marine heart bitter to the taste.

Pathfinder

With our rings as round as the "o" in Galileo
We exchange our nuptial vows, our hearts beating
In close proximity. Our hearts' impact once
Scattered regoliths here on the way to Mars.

Poised in awe like the earth-moon spin,
We observe Armstrong and Aldrin's
Fit footprints on the plain's talcum-sands
Then, deftly inscribed by Apollo and Insight.

Further on from the fossil-riverbed, mascons
Spurt all around us like tuberoses. We cannot
See nor touch nor smell these succulents –

Metaphors are maudlin tools on the moon –
Roses cultivated on earth's irrigated soils
Metamorphosed memorabilia of our origins.

*"Pathfinder" won The Polaris Trilogy Contest
and will be sent to the moon on a time-capsule
by NASA in 2024.*

Barrier-Skin

Gearless, I dived down
the bathos of the Coral Sea
and swam along the coral-atriums.

A mnemonic coral-branch now bleeds
in the interstices of my memory.

From the dim anteroom, they brought in
a bowl of oil to mend my bruises but my blood
fomented until we beseeched

the vellum-book of hours
to graft the primal zoo-colonies
with chlorophyll, imploring the hours

to eradicate the aragonite gnawing
upon the primeval coral shells
down the bare bathos of my gearless dive

where like poison nettle-welts, toxic palythoa
polyps had blemished my barrier-skin
with clotted blood and urticaria.

The Warrants

I will return to the Aegean, the sea
of my youth where dolphins raced after
our departing ship in swathes of light
breaching, jumping, leaping into silver arcs.

The Aegean hides its carnage of flesh
below the surface yet, deep sea-currents
diminish the virulence of the viruses
that tatter our wounded world. I will commune

with the cerulean waves of the Aegean
as waves mingle with the gleam
of that navy-blue and teal mother-sea
where ripples and tides swell the billows

and a plankton-filled potency conducts the currents
through recurrent sun-cycles, our earth's warrants.

The Scavenger-Moon

The Scavenger-Moon

The scavenger-moon bestrewed
the Mediterranean pines into terraced
canopies. Dishevelled the beryl-beach.
You were borne away by the tides
sated by the moon's attraction.
The sirocco poured pine needles
and seeds to the sea. We craved

for one another. A crab's claw and
a herring's spine littered the beach.
The tide, stressed with the sea's energy,
brought you back to me. Connected
by memory-cues, we loved each other.

Rain-water sprouted firs and trees.
Breathing was eased and redeemed.

Scavenger-Lover

My dreams are broken by the greed of your desire.
My eyelids' weigh on my slumbering eyes.
Do you wish to haunt me constantly
to safeguard your image before my eyes?

Like a scavenger, you stalk me, pry into my affairs,
spy on my actions. Yet, my love is fresh as the dew
on the garden grass. I have given you my best bed
covered with silk linen scented with mint and bergamot.

My love shall not admit a scavenger lover
in its bower sheathed with moss-blown branches
to preserve love's balm against suspicion's doubt
to maintain love's harmony against harsh disputes.

Hence, we can live and love like fit lovers
eager to leave the right heir to life's bower.

Horizon

Like the stone-strewn soil of the vineyards
the wine-maker's hands felt callous
to the touch as he handed me the wine glass.
I thought of the winemaker's fieldwork
his outreached wrinkled hands broken
like my porcelain cup crackled along
a straight ancestral line. My tea had hissed
through its broken porcelain pores

across a rare rose specially painted
as a regal reminiscence. The wine
was suffused with the subtle scent of berries,
pepper, cinnamon, and clover. The grapes
coiled like crimson green-ochre ivies
descended towards the lacustrine horizon.

The Convict

The martyr-convict's life-force began
oozing out of her as she repeated
the fake words interjected into her mouth
by the male bigot-judges who condemned her
to an untimely death. Like the beheaded
male mantis sucked for insemination

on the angelica, the convict was seized
by antagonists. The delayed decree
of her martyred life would be enacted
interminably in the movies to reminisce
the crime inflicted on her innocence
reaching beyond her mantis-like death.

Tsunami

Children sing and collect shells, sea-stars,
Tiny crabs hidden within rock-dwellings.

As currents stir the ocean's food-chain
The tide carries flotsam to the shore.

Now the protean wanton-moon surges
Above the soul-sweeping tidal waves.

Traumatic tornadoes ascend the sky, cold
Clouds sweep the air, houses are soaked.

We pray for the moon's orbit to be poised
With the earth's within stabler sky-dynamics.

Actors and Alibis

In quarantine, alibi-shadows
danced in our stead, neglected
our conscious consent.

Confined and censored,
cut were we from the poet's
rhythm, the actor's advice.

Alibi-shadows danced
in our stead, neglected
our conscious consent.

Shadows reeled, reflected
the chiaroscuro extensions
of our daily lives.

We knew, the deadly virus
had its place inside us all
so, we fought Covid's toll –

Slowed down, respected
animals in their own right
kept our houses clean.

Disjuncture

The lucent shield shelters the flesh
of the shell against the sea's deadly
hierarchy. Our greed gnaws on viruses
in infected fish-markets. Fishermen
can no longer hear the earth's elegy.
Widening storm-gyres boost the air-torrents
into tornadoes. Pandemics and water-wars
are loosened upon the valleys of the world.

As we grow vulnerable like children, anger
shreds our skins. We can no longer contain
ourselves. We even grow angrier at each other.

When will we vanquish the rough beast of our anguish?

When we leave the shields of our confinement
We might attain a wiser self-assignment.

Guilt

Self-absorbed as we were
we drove away to forget
our uncouth selves cleft
between committal and neglect.

We drove on ancient roads
to forget our guilt for abandoning
the embattled body
of our loved one locked

in pain like a wounded dog
staggering in a field of debris
limned by broken wheel-tires.

We drove away to forget
the irreparable lack of love
spurted by time's treason.

We left to mend the gap
between our nescience and
the grace of an answer.

Disbelief

Like a baited fish with an opaque
sclera fighting the fisherman hauling his line
mourning was the challenge
I had to vanquish.

Perhaps, the juvenile crows
that bled my head during their breeding
season were foretelling.

non c'è più…non c'è… non c'è… non c'è…

Unexpectedly, came the news
of my nephew's death whom
I was planning to meet in person soon.

non c'è più…non c'è… non c'è…

The river rushed on heedlessly.
Melancholy tarnished my bliss.

My incredulity about his death
benumbed me. Calls to hospitals
in Rome increased my grief.

non c'è più…non c'è… non c'è…

I would no longer honour his invitations
to talk and walk together in Rome.

non c'è…non c'è… non c'è… non c'è…

Sad and detached, he seemed a sheer figure
of light as he laughed with friends in the photos.

non c'è…non c'è… non c'è… non c'è…

A month before his death, I had re-united
with my family, regained my life-gait.
And then, came the dire-day's requiem…

non c'è più…non c'è… non c'è… non c'è…

Life-Force

I moved away
from Love's door
to flee my passion
and the void
of your death

Feeling my mind's
dearth, you said:
"Melancholy is
the body's despair."

With dilated time
I escaped despair
fulfilling love's mission
with my life-force.

The Landmark

We drove between two cities
limned by a river. The river became
the landmark of our desire.

Like a metronome of emotion
the *gymnopédies* resonated
on the car's radio.

Like the car-waves
on the highway, the channelled
river-water was sundered
from the road by bourns.

Van Gogh's potato-eaters
sitting around a dark wooden table
lowly lit by a bare bulb
had delayed the day.

Balsam

On the rare halcyon days of the forest
the spring breeze fluttered on your face
while scented balsams soothed my breath.

As you sought to awaken my inner child,
we were attracted to each other like magnets.
Like iron fillings, your colours became magnetic

fields that almost blinded me. While you raked
the scree off the stone-strewn river, our neglected
trysts repelled our twinned fields. You rebelled

like a procrastinating child and I offered you
my tear-vial. You had understood that distance
and rumours would eventually break us.

Love's Ally

Love's ally, Time, has shown me so much
beauty I can hardly believe to be true.
Love's ally, Time, allures us to beauty
yet steals its perfection with the passage

of time leaving us astonished at Time's flight.
Like the rose, in transience, beauty vanishes.
What can last long enough to be cherished
without being gnawed at by Time?

Our inner values sheathed by true feelings
vanquish Time's usure. Love's false promises
disappear into thin air when our hearts
and souls are reflected in our deeds

like the utter concord of two clock-hands
like the constancy of time-defying brands.

Metamorphosis

Like the poet seeking immortality
through an unfinished manuscript,
Orpheus would not abandon Eurydice

to darkness yet, unbent, she was oozed
into a singularity. Back in Thrace, Orpheus
delved into the mirrors of his buried self.

Like the undertow, his poems poured
through the sea-channels. As Apollo's light seeped
through the olive groves above the cerulean sea

the hills of Elysium echoed with his life-force.

Dispossession

Orpheus listens unknowingly
to broken radio-transmissions,
seeking self-transformation.

He weds Eurydice within a sylvan bower.
Nymphs kindled by envy hound her to Hades
where to Thanatos she remains bound.

Beguiled in Hades by Orpheus' poetry
Sisyphus stops rolling the rock of the furies.
Half-dead rulers are tempered by music.

Like a somnambulist treading
the quagmires of the night, Orpheus'
other-self follows him half-alive.

But Eurydice, then, slips into singularity.
In the olive orchards people sing threnodies.

Orpheus' pastoral pastures
spin-mad like falling dominos.
Melancholy permeates Orpheus.

Yet, as he seeks his other-ego,
Orpheus crosses the Styx
defying Thanatos with his lyre.

Dispossessed, like Orpheus, we forsake
our past initiations. And, despite deceit,
lyricize Eros. In the immensity of the void,
angels beckon us to fare forward.

The Body-Dam

    blood flows
    into our body
      all along
    rivulet-veins

  the body-dam limns
  the psyche-waters
    of the flesh
     corrals
  our inner moods

  avoids the floods
    in the heart's
      interlocked
        chambers

summons our departure

    in the cool of the night
      we polished
    our marble floors
       streaming
      down with
    the sacrificial waters
     of our imminent
       departure

    in the scorched heat
      of two summers
       we cleaned
        the gaps
        between
        the bricks
       of our books

    and departed

The Raft

The Raft

I.

With sailor-knots, the balsa-logs were tied tightly
each to each. Trade winds drifted the raft north
towards the Humboldt. With a square canvas sail
the raft joined the Equator's currents on the West Pacific.
The long-weeded oar and its sculpted pine-blade
steered almost virtually. A seaman held on tightly
to the main sail to protect the thatched bamboo-cabin
against the gales. Like fast flying knives, flying fish
poured onto the deck, supplementing the ton of water,
the brine-bread, and the plankton-porridge.

Sharks were harpooned before they could devour
the sailors alive. Like surgeons, they extracted bile,
flesh, and parasites from the hunt to be tested.

A frigate announced the nearest archipelago.

II.

The barrier reefs were treacherous teeth
that could grind the raft. The elder seaman said
they were to circumnavigate the tallest atoll
through the ebb-and-flow. And they did.
Like their forefathers, they planted calabash
and yam on the beach. Through radio codes
they healed a native boy's head injury.
Like their forefathers, they succeeded
in mastering the accuracy of *guara* navigation.
Like their forefathers, they felt exalted
to have vanquished the protean sea.

The Mask in Sutton Hoo

With molten silver, I shaped a head-
shield that fit an identical iron face,
a regal mask meant for eternity.
For this sculpture, I consulted an iron-

smith who welded the silver mask
to an iron headshield. Like the carved oars
of the ancient war-faring ships, I sculpted
the face with square-striae and symbols.

The king's wars were engraved in relief
on mobile panels. The totem of a golden
sea-phoenix was welded to the headshield
protecting the face. The thick eyebrows

resembled birdwings shielded
by two wolves. Guarded by armed giants,
the amphibian-totem carried away
the sword-bearer to oceanic eternity.

The Albatross

His cornucopia filled with eels, blue cods,
and squids, the fisherman sailed upon
the southern Pacific. He poured the fish
from his woven nets to the wicker baskets
purifying them with a soul-prayer. Like the fish-
totem tattooed on his arm, the foam-feathered
albatross hovered above his boat. The fisherman
let the bird feed on a purified portion of fish.

The albatross glided along large air-shafts
but, no sooner, returned to announce broken
weather. The sea, gradually, turned sepia-brown
with wind-tipped sediment. Yet, swiftly and with wings
of safety, the bird brought the ship through the blizzard
to the port. The albatross became the fisherman's totem.

Cod-Roe

Like primaeval fish preserved
in amber bees-wax, I found *bottarga*
on the market in Porto Vecchio
on the Tyrrhenian archipelago.

The amber-cured cod-roe, wrapped
in ochre bees-wax reminded me
of the *bottarga* my grandfather brought
home from the market – cut into thin slices

on rough toasted wholemeal bread
the golden granules melted
like spiced butter in our mouths.
Soft as ointment on my hands

the bees-wax is reserved
for candle-making – an elegy
sung in polyphony under candle-light
for the peace-probing souls of the dead.

The Life-Tree

After Leonora Carrington's painting

Will I survive the very light
I create as it irradiates from the divine
figure protected by angels?

Cloaked in tawny coats
the philosophers with winged
beasts lying below their feet argue
about the essence of truth.

The divine quintessence
wanes the moon's gleam
lighting up the stars
and nebulae from within.

Would enlightenment emanate
from within like a crystal lamp lit
on a grief-veined night wherein roam
hybrid hyenas, lions, or ligers to objectify
our pent-up passions on paper?

The Dunes

When the car stopped, the jade sea-air
spurred me on towards the huge dunes
on the beryl-beach spreading out
like boulders tumbling down from the hills.

As if hypnotised, I gazed intensely
at the sands budged by the sea-breeze
moving upon the northern sea through
the thick window-panes keeping

the ill winds out of the barrier-resort.
On one dune, there slithered a juvenile
sand-serpent ready to ambush
its predators by burying its body
inside the soft sands stealthily.

A Maritime Battle

With their tensile bodies stretched like a virtual army
across the Orcus straits, predator orca-pods emerged
from the cold Aleutian waters when the sun waned.

The killer-whales surrounded the ship, pushing it
back towards the strait-waters with their steel jaws.
Some orcas jumped upon the outer deck, attacking

the sailors. The sailors sheared the carnivorous orca-
torsos, throwing them back to the sea with some human-
parts still trapped in their steel jaws. Floating flesh-filaments

were pecked by blood-beaked petrels and frigates.
The seamen fought the predator-orcas skin-to-skin.
As the rain washed off the torn flesh and gore from

the deck, the sailors steered the goods-laden ship back
to the high Aleutian waters, exhilarated to have vanquished
the savage orca-army with their strength and will-power.

Synchronicity

I set out to tame the Atlantic
while cruising. I resonated with
the ocean's wide undulations,
synchronous with the moon's attraction.

On the dolphin-watch, the cruise guide
started shouting as he threw out chunks
of chicken to hook-beaked petrels
and frigates out of a tin box, his arms

spanning widely the open sky.
The hysteria of the poultry-fling hid
the dolphins from our sight. After the swim
the sirocco tainted our eyeglasses with ochre dust.

The served picnic remained untouched.

Ambidextrous

Dolphins, though almost blind, hear to visualise
and echo-locate our bones, sinews, and tendrils

through the sonar soundwaves travelling from
their melons towards our bodies through the depths.

An ambidextrous boy was delivered by a mother
through dolphin-play in a pool by the coral sea.

The dolphin matriarch warrants the team's
cohesion and initiates the cubs' lactating speech.

Dolphins play, hunt, migrate to breeding grounds
through magnetic sonar fields linked to the sun.

The Whale's Cradle

In memory of the stranded whale
the sculptor shaped the ship's hull
like the whale's torso, incurved
with oak branches, polished,
and smoothened with bees-wax.
Like a sea-sentinel, he incrusted
the ship's body with lucent shells
to safeguard the whale's cradle
and the sea's protean memory.

The Whale-Way

Plankton and krill are the baleen's
keratin-filtered meal. From the ice-capped
Arctic, satin beluga-pods migrate
towards the south to feed on shrimps,
salmon, krill, and iodine-weeds.
Under the frozen Antarctic speedway
minke-baleens swim, whistle, and play
along the ice-cold ocean. In the depths
baleens squawk, cry, and whisper
to each other. Now, whale-wrath swells
our storm-steered oceans. In future
our eco-endeavours will warrant
the oceans' prevailed whale-trails.

Blind Spots

in cyclic
overturn
cars
like waves
flow
on the highway
with hybrid
energy

as waves
mingle
and move
with the foam-
on-brine
the wind
imprints
my skin
with saline
blind spots

The Abalone Hunt

The full moon ormering tide sways the kelp
forests in the Coral Sea. On the drop-down
from the neritic limn, I measure the limestone
shells with their breathing pores in the selenizone.

The shells that survived the dinosaurs, cling
to their rock-hosts as if they are rocks themselves.
I cut them off from their rock-hosts with
a plastic knife to prevent them from bleeding.

A shock on the coiled Cretaceous spiral and
the snail-flesh secretes a ceramic fluid between
sliding bricks to form a body-armour and a pearl.

On the ground above the aquifer and the water-table,
the convex shell, rough in the hand, yields to iridescent
green-purple-silver swathes of refracted light.

Glimpses of Light

An absence, ethereal as the wind,
yet corporeal as a wound, grips my body.
Images arise from my malleable life-force.

My inner garden's palimpsest, the text grows
like a tended garden, blending song, sinew, and symbol.
Intuition becomes a glimpse of the unknown

from the original knowledge of our wounds.
We, then, see the light that binds our consciousness
to mend our quarantined world.

Chiaroscuro

Her lowered gaze seems as ephemeral
as her bonnet's fleeting shadow upon her *blasé*
face creased like an autumn leaf. Child-like
the painter projected his self-love on
our self-searching Cassandra. She reads
an illuminated book, her guiding shield
against ignorance. Her wrinkled right hand
rests on the lit book depicting her life-experience

in line with the scriptures, protecting her talent
for progress and prophesy. She compensates
for her guilt as a self-conscious feminist. The light's
intensity on her page insinuates Rembrandt's

obsessive quest of immortality after death
strengthened by his alter-ego's feminine faith.

The Lightkeeper

The hologram-token I hold in my hands
now brightens the carved stone-
tower and its arcades, now reveals
the stone-tower's interior – the iron-

wrought handrail, the keepers' quarters,
the turned-on radio, the Zephyr's veering
force on the cloud-bound Atlantic. Further up,
the keeper adjusts the crystal-clean rotator

diffusing a diffracted light on the rippling
coves and the scattered rocks below.
Upon a steep slope, I had, once, subtly

been forewarned of the lightkeeper's Tenebrae,
of a sailor floating upon a coffin-plank,
of the abyssal trenches below and the undertow.

Acknowledgements

"Fluctuations" in *Wisconsin Review,* Volume 53, issue 1, October 2021.

"Sunbathers" *in Mundane Joys*, A Poetry Anthology, Derailleur Press, May 2021.

"The Life-Tree" in San Antonio Review, Volume V (Spring), March 17, 2021.

"Chiaroscuro" and "Glimpses of Light" in *The Quiver Review*, March 24, 2021.

"The Whale-Way", "The Convict", and "The Landmark" in *The Otherwise Engaged Literature and Arts Journal*, Volume 7, July 2021.

"Horizon" and "Actors and Alibis" in *Open Skies Quarterly*, Vol. 6, October 2021.

"Disbelief" in ExTempore, January 2021.

"The Undertow", "Disjuncture", "Life-Force" in *The Otherwise Engaged Literature and Arts Journal*, Volume 8, December 2021.

"Chalk-Hills" in *OxMag,* Miami University MFA, Print Issue 48, Spring 2022.

"Time, A Meditation" in *Literary Heist,* Ottawa, June 20, 2022.

"The Scavenger-Moon" in *"Remington Review"*, July 20, 2022.

"The Abalone Hunt" in *North of Oxford,* August 15, 2022.

"The Raft" in *The Book of Matches,* Issue 6, Fall 2022.

"The Lightkeeper", "Hubris", "Synchronicity", "The Body-Dam", "Challenger", in *Lothlorien Poetry Journal,* September 9, 2022.

"Ambidextrous" in *Poets Live Anthology, Issue 4,* November 2022.

"Dispossession, I" & "Dispossession, II" in *The Otherwise Engaged Literature and Arts Magazine,* Volume 10, December 2022.

"The Warrants" in *The Deronda Review*, Jerusalem, 2022.

"Fragments" in *Contemporary Poems Anthology,* December 2022.

"Barrier-Skin" in *Ballast Journal,* January 17, 2023.

"The Dunes", "Metamorphosis", "The Mask", and "The Sea-League" in *Soren Lit,* February 6, 2023.

"Cod-Roe", and "Tsunami" in *Salzburg Poetry Review, 40,* Spring 2023.

"Pathfinder", in *The Polaris Trilogy* published by Brick Street Poetry Inc. January 23, 2023.

Author's Biography

Dr. Emily Bilman is a poet-scholar who lives, writes, and teaches in Geneva, Switzerland where she is Poetry Society's Stanza representative. Her dissertation, *The Psychodynamics of Poetry: Poetic Virtuality and Oedipal Sublimation in the Poetry of T.S. Eliot and Paul Valéry* with her poetry translations, was published by Lambert Academic in 2010 and *Modern Ekphrasis* in 2013 by Peter Lang, CH. Her poetry books, *A Woman By A Well* (2015), *Resilience* (2015), *The Threshold of Broken Waters* (2018), and *Apperception* (2020) were published by Troubador, UK. "The Tear-Catcher" won the first prize given by *The New York Literary Magazine*. The sonnet "Pathfinder" won the Polaris Trilogy Contest. Poems and translations were published in *The London Magazine, San Antonio Review, The Wisconsin Review, Expanded Field, Poetics Research, The Blue Nib, Tipton Poetry Journal, North of Oxford Journal, Otherwise Engaged Magazine, Literary Heist, The High Window, Wild Court, Remington Review, Book of Matches, Lothlorien Poetry Journal, Poets Live Anthology 4, OxMag, Deronda Review, Contemporary Poetry 2022, Ballast Journal, Soren Lit, Southern Arizona Press Anthologies, Poetry Salzburg Review.*

She blogs on http://www.emiliebilman.wixsite.com/emily-bilman